PRAISE FOR
PROPRIOCEPTION

"C. Prudence Arceneaux's debut unfolds like a taxonomy of desire, ferociously precise in the face of all it risks. *Proprioception*'s resolute muscularity deals in the erotic, esoteric, and ironic alongside the fusions, the refusals, the lyric and literal unrest only an embodied witness, shorn of self-pity, without a thought of folding, could hold in her hand. Few first collections have redoubled my allegiance to poetry's audacity, musicality, and vitality like this one."

> —SUSANNA CHILDRESS, author of *Jagged with Love* and *Entering the House of Awe* and a collection of essays, *Extremely Yours*

"*Fury* is the first word that came to me reading C. Prudence Arceneaux's third collection of poetry, *Proprioception*. Within fury nested the savvy—fun-loving, quick-witted. Within the savvy, an unabashedness, one that challenges the concept of a poem's 'speaker'—of politic—and, finally, cloistered inside them all, a sensuality in acts such as weeding a garden and sharing a lime. Here, Arceneaux is engrossing, demonstrating her awareness for the intimate while highlighting just how interconnected our worlds are, and why we should all share such fury. Stunning."

> —CLEMONCE HEARD, author of *Tragic City*.

"C. Prudence Arceneaux is a brilliant poet of immense *ferocity* & *velocity*. The poems of *Proprioception* move with muscular grace, surprise, and startle, feeling utterly fresh, unlike anyone else's poems. How Arceneaux manages to be wry, sexy, contemplative and rueful all at once, is a wonder. I love the weed pulling! What a gift. Sprung from astonishment, whirling, shifting, pitching a mind into wild new states of being, these poems are *alive*."

> —NAOMI SHIHAB NYE, author of *Everything Comes Next* and *The Tiny Journalist*

PROPRIOCEPTION

PROPRIOCEPTION

POEMS

C. PRUDENCE ARCENEAUX

The Sabine Series in Literature

TRP: THE UNIVERSITY PRESS OF SHSU
HUNTSVILLE, TEXAS 77341

Library of Congress Cataloging-in-Publication Data

Names: Arceneaux, C. Prudence, author.
Title: Proprioception : poems / C. Prudence Arceneaux.
Other titles: Sabine series in literature.
Description: First edition. | Huntsville : TRP: The University Press of
    SHSU, [2025] | Series: The Sabine Series in Literature
Identifiers: LCCN 2024022253 (print) | LCCN 2024022254 (ebook) | ISBN
    9781680034028 (trade paperback) | ISBN 9781680034035 (ebook)
Subjects: LCSH: Time perception--Poetry. | Aging--Poetry. | Well-being--Age
    factors--Poetry. | LCGFT: Poetry.
Classification: LCC PS3601.R3835 P76 2025 (print) | LCC PS3601.R3835
    (ebook) | DDC 811/.6--dc23/eng/20240516
LC record available at https://lccn.loc.gov/2024022253
LC ebook record available at https://lccn.loc.gov/2024022254

FIRST EDITION

Cover art by Brenda Swan
Author photo by Chris Reichman
Cover design by Cody Gates, Happenstance Type-O-Rama
Interior design by Maureen Forys, Happenstance Type-O-Rama

Printed and bound in the United States of America
First Edition Copyright: 2025

TRP: The University Press of SHSU
Huntsville, Texas 77341
texasreviewpress.org

THE SABINE SERIES IN LITERATURE

Series Editor: J. Bruce Fuller

The Sabine Series in Literature highlights work by authors born in or working in Eastern Texas and/or Louisiana. There are no thematic restrictions; TRP seeks the best writing possible by authors from this unique region of the American South.

BOOKS IN THIS SERIES:

Cody Smith, *Gulf*

David Armand, *The Lord's Acre*

Ron Rozelle, *Leaving the Country of Sin*

Collier Brown, *Scrap Bones*

Esteban Rodríguez, *Lotería*

Elizabeth Burk, *Unmoored*

Cliff Hudder, *Sallowsfield*

David Middleton, *Time Will Tell:*
The Collected Poems of David Middleton

Ron Rozelle, *The Windows of Heaven*

C. Prudence Arceneaux, *Proprioception*

Cody Smith, *River Hymnal*

I would like to thank the following for giving these poems homes:

178 (limes)	*Limestone Literary Journal*
Christchurch	*Willow Review*
Crest	*TORCH Literary Arts*
Dear John	*Cathexis Northwest*
Grotto	*KARAMU*
Hurricane Season	*Tiny Seed Literary Journal*
I weed like a woman angered	*Inkwell*
Jesse	*Clark Street Review*
Just Inside the Gate	*Brain Mill Press*
The lady lobster is lucky	*Cathexis Northwest*
language	*Slipstream*
Menopause	*Poem- A- Day*, Academy of American Poets
My Cousin Dies, Like a Deer, on the Side of the Road	*Texas Observer*
Navigation	*Brain Mill Press*
The President did not want to see anything "difficult" at the National Museum of African American History and Culture	*South Florida Poetry Journal*
Retirement	*The Book of Life after Death*
Scorpinacity	*Plainsongs*

TABLE OF CONTENTS

the ability to orient oneself in the world

EVERY DAY

I pledge allegiance to this state of fear,
to arrector pili, and the slight electrocution
of smooth nipple muscles, swear fealty

to the nose that knows Smoke from Flash from
Pepper; to the land where we are delivered Priority,
Fragile: then bubble wrap of our lungs squeezed

and twisted; to this land we crack like communion
wafers, game pieces over magmatics; to the ceremony
of judicial stands, one gasping hope, one year after another,

under the watchful eye of a being who marvels in our red-marbled sclera.

NATURE SHOW: THE LORD OFFERS EXPLANATION

Sir Attenborough believes what he says
      when announcing that the Alguiles Tides
      are the fastest shifting on the planet, but
I can't help thinking what the hell is wrong

with him. Apparently he's never studied
      the precipice of black adolescence, the phe-no
      -me-non, in time-lapse, of the male of species
deliquescing from cute to convict, the female,

how pretty ebbs, prey flows. The good lord,
      seminarial, establishes half-tides, like we aren't all
      half given to the ass-whooping the Moon gives
the Earth; you better believe that is what

happens and no amount of foot-in-the-back
      girdling can control this bulge. Our brain fluid
      has little hope, the full tides of our hearts even less.
What we are studying, anthroapologizing,

is deeper than the Mariana Trench, wider
      than the Cassini Gap, but he wouldn't know
      that since he isn't concerned with black space.
BBC One needs to observe, in a human blind,

set up moonlight cameras, see a system tidally

      locked in hate, police camera traps catch

      the vortices created as brown skin pushes

against armor, pulled to embrace by white arms.

Forget about what you thought you knew:

      armadillos transmitting leprosy, pluralizing *octopuses*

      to *octopi*, and no one has seen $8 trillion stacked. Let's

talk about a gravitational power that could make

the Mississippi reverse its course, stop

      the supply of skins and furs. Imagine waking

      each day, not knowing if you are drowning, if you are

sandbarred, if you are undertowed, if you are pipelined, underrolled.

The production must be air- gapped, though; reality

      is just another version of historical publication.

      We don't really need another old white man telling

us the science of our sex, of our race, but maybe

if the voice has a British accent, you'll listen, you'll believe.

Each summer, 500 million 3 inch worms blackhead the pores
of glacial faces. Scientists don't understand it, but don't call it crazy.

"Fascinating," "scintillating"—that's what you are. Worthy
of study. But you've had the narrative arc all wrong.

The main character: man or woman or water bear: just dies. No cancer,
no tragic falls, no consumption, no rickets, not drunk—Just stops

being, and no one cares. At the corner of N41°43′32 and W49°56′49,
there's a room of velvet, brocade and satin, bespoke in liquid black,

symphony-full: bodies, strings, organs. A cellist's forearm in lunar tempo.
No need to change the history—of course they played while the ship

dervished to the floor. If you were about to be rewombed in cold amnion,
wouldn't you want your last thoughts to be of the first time you realized

you could please yourself, with concentration, practice, and the movement
of pressured fingers? Why's it have to be crazy? What if your blood

is supposed to be blue. What if the connection between bone and tendon
is supposed to be broken, bones dissolved, besotted, malunioned.

What if sound only travels through a rictus of agonies.
What if—just what if—you aren't supposed to come up for air.

HANDS DOWN- A PANTOUM

For the practice of life, we held hands.
Our heads thrown back—in the dust—our words lost.
We sheltered what we thought was the most important,
what a heart holds, what a heart says with

our heads thrown back—in the dust—our words lost
the malleable, the gentleness, the ability to shape our world,
what a heart holds, what a heart says with
what we believe to be true sifting through the air.

The malleable, the gentleness, the ability to shape our world
seem just beyond the reach of small fingers, small hands hold
what we believe to be true sifting through the air,
through our unskilled hands, it smelled like perfume. This loss

seemed just beyond the reach of small fingers, small hands hold
sheltered what we thought was the most important.
Through our unskilled hands, it smelled like perfume, this loss.
For the practice of life, we held hands.

while we swish antidepressants into the toilet bowl, like ice
in a gin & tonic, we overmedicate the waters for a 5 mile sewer center,

waves of Paxil and Zoloft, Cymbalta lap over frogs, snakes, fish, crawdads,
so numbed they forget who they are—timid morsels—swagger from
their mud chalets, no fear in evolutional security. The one whose

head you're sucking, overdosed on Celexa, not enough to make him fly,
but enough to shake your hand. Mice, brave like grackles, now
negotiate halving your sandwich before leaving with 3/4. Do you

remember the first time you heard the sun would explode, the dog nails
on hardwood skittering of your heart? This is where we are, training
with aversion sensory input. Commercial facts do a steady 160

marathon rhythm in my head—only 9% of your washed and dried
plastic gets recycled, Ghana doesn't want any more Old Navy 4th
of July t- shirts, for only 200 monthly payments of $19.95 you can

have a knife handled with wooly mammoth bone. Isn't there a garbage
utopia floating in the Pacific? The perfect place for fictosexuals, all the
materials there to build condos, always by the seashore. We discover it

as New Atlantis, create a geomythology that teaches it has always been
thus. With you, and also with you. Billy Collins is reading poems
on the radio while I'm driving; I can't put my head down. I'm still woozy

thinking of the oligarch playing Cat's Cradle with mastodon DNA

in Siberia (Buy your knives now; soon you can only handle sabre tooth)

and Billy's intonation syncopates on the back of my eyeballs, each

mallet jukes my gall, a bile reflux. Like premature Spring here. Flowers

bloom, plants fruit; they'll die, a fifth cold front, this time in July. Or

maybe what kills them are his false analogies, like Betta—too far from

their pond, not near enough to another to pick a fight. Billy speaks with

the voice of Job. This story, I know! He loses the she-asses, the shrouded

servants, the camels, the lambs, the wheat, the grass, the ears of attention.

And maybe this time the god isn't handing out consolation prizes.

I WEED LIKE A WOMAN ANGERED.

I plant my feet, warrior stance.
I don't even know what I am grabbing, yanking, tearing from the earth.

I didn't plant this bed. Anyone looking at it
can tell it was laid by a man.

He dug up sheets of grass and dirt,
turned them over in his hands, and put it all right back,
without once checking to see what was going in to
the bed. There was no look for the seeds of ugly things,
the stuff that comes back, unwanted.
He placed the new plants, fresh shoots, green with life,
in that dirt, and stood back to watch his work.
Stood back and walked away.

He promised to water, to feed, to take out anything
that would only hurt the life there. Promised
and walked away. So here I am, in the sun,
hunched like an old maid, getting out the things
he overlooked, the things he can't be bothered to notice.

Anything with spines scares me. The bees deter me;
until they go about their business elsewhere I am frozen,
the garden gnome among the green. I think these are aphids I crush
as I move from tiny pecan tree to tiny budding pecan tree.
I have to take breaks to look up what I pull out of this bed:
Johnson grass, Crab grass, clover.
And I am enthralled by my pulling. Until I pull some thing
that should be there, in this garden.

But I remember it was laid by a man
who doesn't know how to care for a bed.

I weed like a woman angered.

Because I am.

WHORES LIKE US (OR, IF THAT'S WHAT YOU CALL "WHORES")

I want to be a whore like Mary Magdalene—
light footed, full armed, my hair probably
my best feature, my breath heavy perfume

because I love the feel of those small onions
in my mouth when I bite down, like grapes, musky.
The men come and pay their rent to me, as I wait

in the shadow of my sitting room, and as they come,
dropping coins into the bowl, I wait in shadow.
But when he comes I switch to the mint leaves,

fumbling for the bowl, tripping over my own hair,
on my knees before him; it's how the rumors start.
            But to be a whore like her, it doesn't matter because

he comes to her, comes to me, to hide from the others,
to hide from those who drain him as the midday sun.
And after a day of waiting in the shadows, when he comes

to me, he only asks, "Please don't make me speak."
I want to be the kind of whore men who have never had me
make rumors about: how I writhe, I howl, how I let them treat

me like they would the little girls they watch, fresh-skinned
and wet-lipped. Their eyes follow me the same way. I want them
to tell stories of me, for years, of how I sinned in their eyes, and know

that it is the smell of my hair they wished lingered on their chests,

the taste of my mouth, raw and honest, which settled on their tongues,

they wish the skin he'd touched was soft in their hands.

At this point there are no   beans
to warm my stomach and the   echo
of its loneliness seems to   vibrate
out from my fingers to lie   like
a stain on every surface I   touch
waning in any light   holding
a smell of its own that   misplaces
sound around it appearing like   heat
waves that can only make it   seem
that I am less hungry and only   more
interested in the   hunt

I found myself stopping at the treeline
on the mountain. My breath gray, forming
shapes that look like me for a momentbut something
like what I'll seem in yearsto come, stooped and heavy in most places.I
placed my back against the trunk ofa tree, little more than a flaking pole,and
stared at the ground two inches fromthe new rubber of my shoes. These trees didn't
want to cross this imaginary line made by soft brown earth and blurringinto a color
of stone, wet and crumbled.They didn't want to be there and I waitedfor my eyes, skin, legs
to register that I didn't want to be there either. I'dheard it was to be a sea of moving
buoyant gray and I could see all the waydown, further than where I'd started,
farther down than anything needed to beand at some point down there, it all
cametogether, like a seam I've sown, fat and lumpyin most places, but in others,
where itseems most crucial, whatever holds thisall together was too thin and
sparse. Iwanted to test the butterfly effect here,beat my wings, stamp my
feet to watchit all shake and crack and shearbut from here breathing is
the hard part and I know that if I thought about it,I would realize it is
my heart shaking the treenot the wind. I looked at the ground be
fore my feetand know why the trees stopped where they did.
This high, it's enough to receiveair, to work to get life
from what is suspended above and around. To
movethose two inches would mean more
work,a justification to failure. The
trees know best.

DEAR JOHN

Every woman should have a man like you.
    A married man who treats her
    like another man's property, always
    careful to not show signs of wear, signs of use.
    A man who brings the smell of another woman
    when he rustles between her thighs, so
    heavy she can taste the first in his eyes, his hair.

Every woman needs a man like you. A man
    who will teach her about animals
    and fear, show her how to gently expose
    the white-white of her eyes. With you, she will
    learn to smell fear. How it is damp and sticky,
    muggy and runny, like the last days of a period—
    the important waiting for no thing. Show her
    how the smell starts under her scalp, then
    it is under her nose, so she can smell
    her own body posturing.

A man like you will teach her to be afraid,
    scenting the air for the smell he brought
    to her bed. Your kind can teach a woman
    to speak in whispers because she must speak,
    but you lower your voice.

And a woman requires a man who will teach her to fear drink.
      Show her the lip of a beer bottle, so like
      the smooth lip of a man's penis. Train her to hold
      the bottle just so in her hand, just so in her teeth.

A woman must have a man like you who compares her
      to another woman, who says his wife's golden hair
      is nothing like the brown bleed of her skin, contrast
      his wife's clocklike moans to her musk groans. A man
      like you will confide these things, make a woman's skin move
      to the words. You will treat her like your wife, only
      ten years ago, and allow a woman into a fantasy she never knew
      she wanted. She will faint in her own disgust.

A woman deserves a man like you. A married man
      who shows her how to undo her weave, slowly
      and gently, thread by thread, as if each section
      she'd finished had been wrong all along, with no more
      attention to the process than he gives his wife. And when
      the pieces bound by her blood and spit are reduced
      to a void of thread, she will remember the fat sky
      and lazy clouds you both lay under and remember
      that a man like you will remind her of all she
      sacrificed for what neither would call "love."

SUPPER

This egg drop soup is corn-heavy, and I am drunk
on salt, my stomach an ocean at low tide.
There is a constellation of clouds flung in the bowl,

my fortune, what lies, written in green onions.
Pictures look like this; the lines seem clear, but we don't
know what happens with the hand behind the back,

the half of a body on the edge. And there are pictures
we see, and pictures never taken. We remember the moments—
or think we do—and our pictures change.

I drink down this bay—we are here an hour—spin my bowl
again, cold fortunes. His nail bitten quick. He watches me,
skirts me, like a wild dog.

after reading *The Happiest Man in the World*

To be clear—he never asked her to live
in a tent or on a boat. But she could feel it coming:

the way he shuttered his eyes at random times
during the day, their bright green fogged,

like the blinds on the windows, the lids
had to click four, five times to distinguish

her brown skin from the brown sheets of his bed,
her face from the smudges of everything else.

The uneasy quake when she entered or left
the trailer, in retrospect, seemed like training

for the unsteady heave of tides. She realized
at some point she no longer noticed, her weight,

her gait adjusted, she realized she no longer cared
whether or not the neighbors could see

their naked shadows cross the windows, whether or not
they ignored the list, the creak when she stayed the night.

She figured they were all out to sea in the trailer park.
But he showed her land once. Behind the wheel

of a truck, one hand on the back of her neck,
he drove with purpose, leagues from the familiar,

following the sun star, his thumb rubbing
a biology lesson on her spine, then harder still;

the knotty bones—a worry stone. He spoke of "grass";
she remembered not to correct him: "weeds."

He offered her food: tomatoes, overripe, fluerdels
recurled, still growing; slow finger circles help peaches

free of skin; they gnawed meat from rib bones, laughing
as she wiped her face with her wrist. He eyed her wistful.

Yet every time she stepped up to the mast of him,
he stepped two states away, until there was no more land.

Then when there was no more water, stepped into the sky.
She waited, for a time, for him to fall from the dark—

    eclipsing moons, shooting stars, solar flares—all the signs.
This is her test of endurance; she stands in the night,

knees locked, shielding her eyes as if from a bright light,
to see if she could find him, because surely if he didn't tumble

back to her, he must still be there. She knows he's gone.

But she can't help herself.

THE LADY LOBSTER IS LUCKY,

she gets to pee
everywhere [fanning it, so to speak]. It is
the evolution of humans that these events—
urination, showers of gold—are things to be
hidden, however accidental. She doesn't
have to pause in her thought, inevitably
forgetting about the he-lobster there
and instead the he-lobster who was there—
bigger claws he had, maybe? A reaction time
like a mantis shrimp?—She doesn't have to worry
about who will lie in the wet spot. Does she have
the option to decide how to molt? Head first? Feet
first? Or does it simply start unbidden, the dilation
of pupils when the human male stretches the smell
of his sweat like old soil, still fertile, still
waiting. Does she watch him posture as she elbows
out of the old man? Or does she back out of the past:
the foot she lost in haste, limb bud fleshy and full
of phantom story, why style the tiny hairs of her tail only
to have swimmerets crushed? How long until color returns?
Does she flush red at the thought of her new he-lobster
or play coy, leaving him wondering who all this stripping,
peeing is for? No matter. He stays, waits. What takes
her thirty minutes, takes a human female thirty years.

LANGUAGE

he frowns when i say *penis*, works me
like a child, through words that rhyme
pick   brick   stick.
he says it's simple to say:
          dick.
he says *i* say it too hard.
yet his *penis* moves against my leg.

we lay there at night. into the skin
of his neck, i say i want *this* (moving
his hand to my nipple) or *that* (the other
hand to my inner thigh). he reminds me
i never say *what* i want.
i tell him there are no words
that rhyme with *pussy*.

i see the smile of his eyes, his lips
disappeared beneath the dark of my hair.
my hips rise. he says into me,
you must ask for what you want.

i don't hear the rest.

morning light funnels into this room.
the cats wander circles to be fed.
his breathing is irregular but i know
there is sleep; his fingers cradle
the soft sack of his balls.

i look at those closed eyes
silent, moving, and practice this language
the *oh*'s and hard *c*'s and soft *e*'s
and i take in the steady hump
of the *d*, bounce it on my tongue,
the stiff angle of the *k*, upright tense.
i practice the words i must learn
to keep a place in this bed.

The nature of that

                            kind of relationship?

That's taking us past *Habilis* and into *Australopithecus*—solidly on two
feet. I want someone to call me *devastating*. Not the way your

friends do, crying the first time meeting me, how relieved and exhausted
they are—marmots on cliff's edge, debating predation

versus suicide, waving- weary "Pleasure to meet you." I'm thinking more
the way UV rays strip mine the fovea; *devastating* like

the Good Samaritan—not afraid of a lawsuit—truncheons your trachea with
a roadside Bic pen; like the multi- tool can open

er at your femeral artery: It doesn't matter why it's there; I want to know
what I can paint for you. Puppies? Arrows? Sinus rhythms

, maybe—an interactive art? Tell me about me. I promise I'm always as
king with real sugar kisses—nothing sucralose or sorbitol in my

system: Tell me what I did. Imagine your answer leaving us *genu valgum*
when your wordy breath thrusts the air. There is no thing

different about your blood—not boiling or raging—but imagine it pumped
up and out and

                            reddening with desire.

SCORPINACITY

For three days now I've been circling this scorpion.
In the morning, with incorrect eyes, I note its position,
say, three o' clock; by noon, it is at five. It flexes
its tail like an arm, a show of strength, the poison
in its sting just as painful, whether its dying or not, which
could be when it reaches seven or ten or tomorrow. By
evening I circle closer—a buzzard over this carrion. I think
this may have been the one that tapped my wrist in my sleep,
tattooing my veins red flames—watch the tail curl in
slowly, like a machine, then a dying breath
it unfurls; the click of the tip on the floor, an unsteady heart
rhythm. It will be days actually before it stops moving, and
weeks still before I sweep up its body.

My mother has surgery in five days. It could be her foot. Or
woman things. My sister knows the 6am intake schedule,
prepped her home for a three-week convalescent stay.
My sister will be the last face our mother sees, she will hold
our mother's hand, squeeze it, tell her we love her.
I have the will, and I stay where I am, three hours
away. Plenty of time, I think, for everyone to get to my mother's
side, I think, should I be called upon to do the one job my mother
wants me to do, knows I—and not my sister—can do.

MENOPAUSE

For further reference: I go to love
like a fire engine to a three-alarm,   flashing

and spinning, yelling across town. Nothing
to be afraid of: the ceiling falling,   windows

concave, doors bowed and stiff. My body
parts fall to, like I was made   of heat.

Everyone watches, chest-clutching, pointing.
Inhalation will surely be the cause of   my death.

Urban myth says an aging vagina once
well-used will shrink from lack   of exercise.

I would think, instead, like the collar of a sweater,
stretched, gaping. Or a fish out   of water,

grasping for purchase. A soft pop every time
you check to see whether or not   it is dead.

I want a song to be written about me: black
pearls, sulfur, bronze-plated silver.   It should

have a verse about blood-soaked hands,
a chorus that is a shout of   *AAAAAHHHHH!*

[Sing it with me: *AAAAAHHHHH!*]

It won't be a song where someone stares into
lit windows from the end of a driveway   on the last note.

The lime's juice seems sweetest at dawn.
We've brought three to chew and suck,
to bring the sun dragging above
the lines of grasses ahead of us.
Warmth is like a dream lost before
I open my eyes. The earth finally sapped
its store of heat and blazing vapors.

He leads me across this bridge
where we have lost words, thrown
stones, where we have whispered
and cried for the joy of each
other's bodies—all on this creaking wood.
The thin line of water
hisses, excuses itself past the piles
and reeds.

He holds his fingers out, cupping the fruit,
careful of the blade cutting deep into the
green middle. The wind blowing around
our legs and arms picks out
the drops of juice falling from his nails,
from the tip of the knife.

I accept my half of lime, imagine I see
the drops float out across the meadow,
gloss the gray dirt, cradle themselves in blades
of grass, spot a web strung between rocks.

I have been eating and not thinking,
the juice sliding down my arm
collecting in a wet stain in the cloth of my pants.
I flick the liquid from my forearm with the tip
of my tongue and find that he is watching me,
a bit of pulp holding tight to the corner of his lip.

He reaches his foot to the hair of water,
breaking its lazy surface. The sun seems to carry
a haze, pretending that it pushes the cold away,
that it will make us strip down to whatever makes
us base and human. Closing my eyes, I wait for his
fingers to find a home in mine.

I forgot to tell you about the dream I had last
night. Somehow we agreed to go to
someone's wedding, and kept trying to find
ways to avoid talking to other people. At
one point you lit three cigarettes in your
mouth, your lips ∴ like the back burner of
a jet engine.

At another point, I slowly
pressed my face, tongue flat-lap,
into a plate of cake and icing,
while staring into people's eyes
over the edge of the plate.

Trying to find something we could
not argue about, Papi and I talk
about the best way to whistle grass.
The cornfields dry and gray, we round
the Sugar Shack, spittle strung from
my hand, a waste as he checks the land
for its ability. Watching the chicks
peck the dirt I am reminded of the feeling
of chiggers burrowing under my
skin.

In the heat, his t-shirt clutches the
W of his neckbones, the yolkyellow
of his skin staring back at the sun.
He's scratched his head under his cap, two fingers,
and wandered to the road, waving in
afterthought at trucks and cars, check
ing the posts and wires of the bound
ary fence. I veer to the old tree snaked
with rope from swings no longer
swung, the fillets of worn rubber buried in dirt.

Kicking off my shoes I rubbed the
tread clear, from the sole of my foot
I have a feeling that someone was
buried there in the patch of trampled earth,
a soldier of a lost war, a baby girl
missing bones, missing shape.

I turned my head to Papi and
opened my mouth to speak. He'd lit a cigar which
he merely puffed for the aroma of
leaves and mud, and cocked his head to look
beyond me with his blood and
cream eyes. I looked at my dust covered feet
and shut my mouth.

RETIREMENT

I don't believe in God, the Father Almighty.
I do wonder where my father is right now.

Today, the sky, Maximum Blue, colored with a five-year-old's
missed strokes, the starling in the bushes shouts—then growls—a bee
surprised by its wing.

                                    I'm weeding. Again.
I want to believe it will stop, but even in drought,
they punch up. Defeated, I stretch my back and remember
my father's pleasure at this task, his body long as my shadow,
hunched to the dirt. I wonder if he found a job there—where there is.

If when he showed up, he said, "Put me to work."
If he tends gardens, if they have gardens.
If he puts in a full day's work, an hour for lunch,
if he "lazy asses" at the others who sit in that otherly light.
If he turns from his dark words to his bear-like hands
and gently covers a new seed.
If he needs to do this to think he deserves a rest.

WHEN ASKED HOW I FEEL NOW THAT I'M ON LEXAPRO

1

Imagine a line—horizontal.

It goes from there to here.

Then bisect it with another line

—vertical. I let you pick the angles.

Bear with me, please;

we are graphing a life:

nounly, verbly, reflexively, participly.

I now care 35.53% less than I did.

I already cared 63.82% less than other people.

I'm just our side of dead.

I gloam about, clouds like Stevie Nicks scarves

waving from my arms. Days are newspaper gray.

I avoid the color inserts; they all burst red: candy

apple, cerise, tomato, amaranth, cinnabar, fire

brick, vermillion, lava, tomato, lipstick, fire engine.

Can't even look at the comics anymore.

2

You should work at the grief in you, like pick to hurt tooth,
digging metal in again and again, seek the meat, the pulp.
And pace yourself.

The first thrust against the rot will walk
breath from your mouth. You'll stop. Don't
wipe the tears when you start again. This is a fluid business.

If you were in your person clothes, you would note
the absurdity of this choice, but you are in your skin
clothes; don't think much, overly long.

Do what a doctor would do.
Dig in again, seek the edge of the root,
are you too afraid to commit?

Practice sounds you make—
groan, whimper, shriek, moan, scream.
It is unseemly to make a show of yourself.

Remember: you are not a doctor.
There is no doctor to cure this.

South Carolina joins the three states who've gone
back to the use of a firing squad, proclamation fladry
behypers us to no end in jagged parades. Our color
guard of humanity deadsticks some of the execution;

we glidestep when needed, mark time always. We declare
ourselves uncogged from the machine, but still manage to
queue for target practice in the grocery store, the quakes
of our strings undulate past 73 kinds of cereal, 24

types of tampons, fifty types of pink salt. People have started
saying *new quooler* again. The young are afraid of *work*.
The Gulf of Mexico is a sacred space. Its heart beat plumbed
daily. There aren't enough bodies there to compete

with The Middle Passage, so Disney implants statues on the ocean
floor off the coast of Clearwater, like they're priceless deCaires
 Taylors: white sands, white faces. The world isn't that small for
it to be true. They could, instead, sift the sands, raise the architecture.

Saltwater doesn't dissolve what we have grown in the marrow,
only burns when we have stripped away skin. It was all dumped;
they were thirsty as they died with swollen tongue bones. Being
lost is an event. Being dead deserves a gender reveal.

We measure intervals at arm's length, and barrel rulers we watch like rats. They can't vomit, these word promisers, mistaking their inherited inability for a misery balm: choke, roll, flail, choke— that's how we are supposed to die right?

TRYING TO FALL ASLEEP IS LIKE TRYING TO HAVE AN ORGASM

Most days I'm too damn tired.

Blue light and gamma rays play
PONG, with neutrinos in my poor-

mouth Hadron Collider of a skull, its hedonistic point

of adjustment mesospheric. I could

buy aides: balms, massage
oils, lavenders and honeys, eucalyptus

and amber, pillows that title the pelvis, other pillows

lift the knees. But it feels like a thing

that should be natural. Pores alternate
sweat and oils, an extrusion, a cough,

a saturation of the cheeks, the expenditure of electrolytes.

[Put "new sheets" on the list.]

Water helps every thing. Must
remember machines that make

things moist, mists, all night long. It helps regulate breathing.

Do it naked. How many times

have you woken up wrist trapped
in elastic band, thumb warm,

tingling, forearm strapped, tricep tight. Sleep is a kind

of skin hunger; without it, we are

single-celled. My thoughts burn
dirty at 4:59am—heretical, bedoozled,

groutier, turgid. I think of booking a room at The Bed

and Breakfast at Plantation House to see

how I'm serviced. Iron bit served
as supplement for the main course?

A woman asks if I know women hear the footfalls

of different genders differently. Which

sounds of drums? Which of high hats?
Does a *they* thunder? And why does

the amplitude of soundbreaks of this woman's hips

crash my ears like the seashore. I am

walking too close to her, drafting;
I think she misheard my steps. I want

to tell her watching her walk is like hydroplaning.

NASA NEEDS POETS

What I wouldn't give for the chance to sail the void—
I'd let myself get yawed, learn more languages (I am

already fluent in English and Grief.), learn how
to vomit in a bag, to shield myself from too much light.

I've trained my whole life to live in confined space.
But I'll settle for being the first to talk up the musky

promises of terran land under Grand Canyon-red Martian
skies, debate on CNN which atmosphere is most toxic: Venus

or Earth. Oh, to be a meteorologist of Jupiter! Surely, even
I can be right 30% of the time.

Stargazer that I am, a title I'd nametag even were I naked. I'm
sure I should know names and distances but I'll gladly quilt

degrees and magnitudes on the inside of my eyelids. I'll start
every poem with the image of the star-eating

black hole, burping four million tons of life stuff, silently
shouting heartbeats and future tense. Truly, I was born

with an understanding of the subtleties of darkness,
and a need to know: Can you see hate from space?

I want to proclaim the truth of dark matter. Yes, your lord said,
"Let there be light," but there is so much more that is dark,

terrifyingly simple, not knowing what is true North other
than what we've said, of "We have been wrong." "Again."

To be the harbinger of our savage hunger when we make it
to Europa and taint its amniotic seas, extoll the paths of dark

energy that weave through the light, making highways, making
signposts, we should follow! Does it matter what Pluto is

if we don't know what we are? Makemake whispers revelations
in my ears! You'll see—they'll want me be on the payroll

as we expand into the never ending never ending never ending never

the quality of water is different here
feels different from the years i remember.
maybe time away has made me think
the water i drankin colorado that filled me
in new mexico that passed onin san antonio
is nothing more than a reminder that
for a time we were resourcepressed like grapes
provide nourishment, slack thirsts.
and maybe all along this is why idon't drink
water. it doesn't have the taste of home
indigo lands, chewed- up by sugar cane,
white black men in yellowed shirts, muddy
kneed chinos. like a long distancecall, this
water tastes of candle light weeping as cold
sets in thisroom enclosed by the rising sun
under a thick layer of scattered
hurricane scarred cloud.

three pairs of underwear

five pairs of socks

can opener

Other states don't want Texans.

Other countries don't want Americans.

Who wants black people?

ultrathin jacket

crank radio

work gloves

passport

Your mother moved in last May. You've been packed for years.

You don't tell her, didn't want her mouse-like. She sleep-

screams when fear vacations with her.

two toothbrushes

first aid kit

water bottle

pepper spray

You bought rain ponchos the day after they murdered Breonna Taylor.

deck of cards

map of texas

meds

wax pencil

The persistent season in your gut belches warnings this will happen

at night. You don't close your eyes until the sky is watercolored

some lighter shade of awareness.

a comb

granola bars

toothpaste (make that two)

matches

The law says throw away a driver license when it expires.
You have four. Put one in your bra, one on your sole
in your sock, one in your underwear. In case someone
tries to remove who you are.

rice

water purification tablets

two pairs of jeans

ammo

You want to ask her to pack. The rusted rigor of your sleep
is soundtracked with wet belts on her soft neck, the knock
of her temple on concrete, the repeated gurgle of her throat
blocked by her own breath.

space blanket

hat

book of edible plants

knife

When Dad died, she cleansed the house of him. Seed
and hammer, suits and shoes, ashtrays and beer cans.
You kept his pocket knife.

pack of condoms

gun

rubber bands

jerky

She'll sugar-ant when it happens, suddenly concerned

with the provenance of a shoe horn, rubber ducky, glass
pitcher, plastic hanger. It won't be the last time you wonder
how you'll live or how you'll both die.

four gold coins

watch

tea

magnet

You are prepared to barter with your body.

two black t-shirts

beans

flashlight

rope

mirror

She doesn't sense the way the air pants. You ask her
to strengthen arms, legs. 75 years of knowledge, heavy
in her bosom. At least her cane can be a weapon.

glow sticks

oatmeal

sun screen

glasses

You know you will forget your glasses. You can't see,
you won't look. It will be your history. If anyone hears it.
That you couldn't see your salvation right in front of you.

salt

lighter

compass

black sweatshirt

soap

Humans can live for a week without food.

Humans can live for three days without water.

How long can a human sustain on fear?

Hurricane Alicia was the first named storm of the 1983 Hurricane season. For almost 20 years this Category 3 storm held the record for damage costs. The name Alicia was retired.

There is a certain black:

a whispering kind of darkness amplifying
sounds and smells   dreams of light drawn
in shaky hands   the damp sheets have slowly
found a way to the blackened floor   cooling
in the five inch gap to the hardwood   the pulse
of the smallest finger pumps out the seconds
steady grip on the corded edge of the mattress
day and night will continue as one   the alarm
will not signal the dawn   nor will it be necessary
to draw attention to the twenty minutes of peace

CHRISTCHURCH

"This is the most important church in all of Ireland."
We opened our eyes wide, fools, the first
 four times we heard that, but by this time,
we mouthed the words, comic straight men to the irony.
 And these church stops made no sense, for me
or for Heather. Yet we stopped—
the knight's death mask, the cobbled floor, the skim of sheep
shit on our pants.

But when we got to that one—you know, the one in Christchurch—
I found a stained-glass heaven.   Don't laugh.
In that light I understood the idiotic devotion of the cherubim.
We are told Heaven is white, but I stood awash in red,
and I knew. This red stroked me, birthed me, hastened me.

Heather called my name, and I smelled the horse's wet shoulder,
the old priest's wool, but I knew I was the *why* of it all—
made of lead and sand and light.

i was outside for an hour, pulling prairie grasses, weeds

ya know, the serious knee high ones, that sway like windmills in the
   wind,

but still splay out like a whore's legs.

put my back into the pulling, two-handing it.

they each gave that scrunchy-squelchy sound.

knocked the dirt from their greedy ass root balls, like breaking a
   chicken's neck.

it all made me salivate.

so I kept doing it.

ass crack hanging out and all.

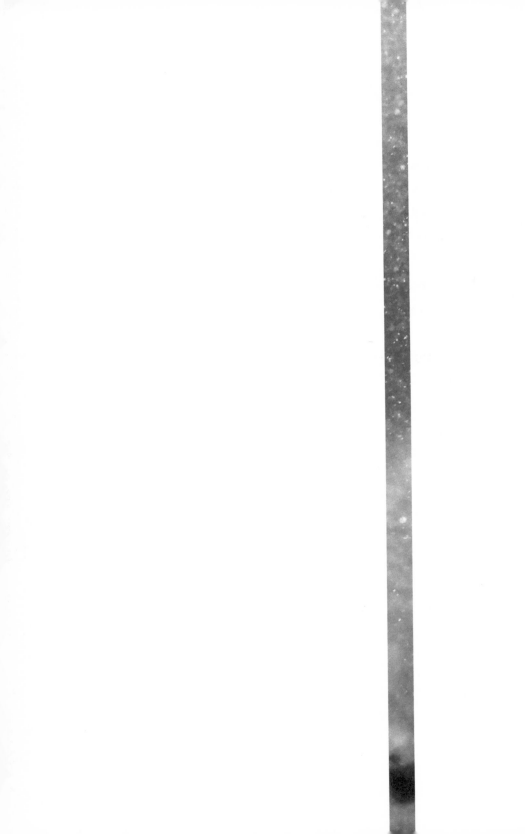

The house across the street is backlit by morning shine, the Earth
tilted against the celestial plane. Farmdogs beyond the reclamation
pond, howling roosters, sunrise in black and gray. The house next door
is guarded by grackles; they lateral line north, west, then north again.

If you'd trusted the griot in your blood, you would have understood the
plague of frogs, as foretold, but they were miniature, desiccated. And if
you'd ever believed in a grimoire, you could have read the loopy cursive
the ants marched out of the chalky ink from those amphibian husks.

You warn the black mothers about what they put in their mouths:
*It's in your milk—the sorrow—settles into the bones of your young. The
government feeds it to you,* you say, *in thick blocks, like cheese.*

But you also missed the dying of the maroon mums. Sure, it was
difficult to tell, their color already so like dried blood, but you
remarked on how they seemed to be supporting each other, falling in
together as a group.

Rittenhouse is unshackled to pledge to the rapiest mix of Greek
letters, oozing poison slurp from his infected gut, keratinized spines
immature, but present. Alex Jones and Steve Bannon scholarship him
into Public Life.

You are studying your 5th degree burns when your nephew texts you at
2 am. He's watching a video of a video of police beating a black man
in 1992. You know he is holding his newborn in one hand, her mouth
newpink and nipple-ready, brain dizzy in formation, as he tries to text
you with the other, his eyes blinking a Morse code of lividity.

You choose to splinter your fingers
pulling up the floorboards
of your home to hide, turn to page 24.

You choose to place just your
third finger against the glass when
you drive by a white person, turn to page 2.

You choose to believe it's ok now,
to worry
about the "little things,"
turn to page 64.

HE RETURNS TO MASTURBATING NOT REALIZING I HAVEN'T FALLEN BACK ASLEEP

Rather than ignore the rumors that it's dangerous to swallow
seeds, I've lived my whole life with the thought that watermelons
the size of thumbnails could be lining my throat, like ticks.

I've swallowed the seeds, white and black. Never was warned about
strawberries, though—each yellow crunch, cracking open potential
in my body. After all these years I imagine my belly verdant, jammy reflux.

***

The largest organ is the skin.
Everyone gets that wrong—on
Jeopardy!, in Trivial Pursuit.

                                 People guess it's the heart, the liver—
 proclamations of Middle Ages
humorists. We are earthquake
sparks, fibers, sacs of goo—cured
in a wet nap.

***

"Straight, with a touch of gay," her ex-wife called me,
        pointed at a closet and yelled, "GET OUT AND STAY OUT!"

***

When a stranger coughs in your face, you think of the ways fear can be measured:

Kilometers

Parsecs

Dols

Kilos

Lumens

Amplitudes

Inches

***

"Where will I be when you realize how beautiful you are?"
Far away, I hope, is what I thought. The eyes were backwash
full. I can't stand weak drunks. But it was sweet.
I miss pick-up lines.

***

13 is my

lucky nu

mber. I d

on't play

it on poni

es or chur

ch raffles.

It's just a n

umber that

never caus

ed me any

worries. P

ut it on a

Friday, s

till noth

   ing.

***

Everyone is so focused on their hands these days. It's erotic,

really: rubbing washing lotioning rubbing lotioning washing /

frictioned hands whiten, pleat, like mannequins', mittened to the wrists.

***

It started:

      The sky smells of fire,

      stars pulled down,

      we tear in their heat,

      smokefogeddy in breath.

      The world sounds of battle,

      happy freedom.

Someone saved these words from me.

***

How is it that this is what we decided to
show
our desire for each other: the pressing of
lips,
the opening of mouth as if for a sneeze or a
yawn,
the swabbing of another's inner cheeks with tongue?
We
wonder at dogs because they sniff each other's
anuses,
in greeting, learn to know the truth of the
other
through what they've eaten or excreted. I've
often
said we should be more like dogs, nose to
glands,
teeth to neck; we'd waste less time on
fools.

***

Scientists now say they can use cat DNA and dog DNA to aid in murder
investigations. Can you imagine Fluffy called to avenge his mamma?
Think of it—when will someone breed a dog that shoots DNA like quills
 or from lizardy eye sockets? Always loyal, always there for you.

***

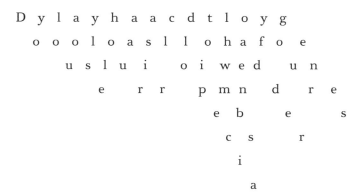

D y l a y h a a c d t l o y g
  o o o l o a s l l o h a f o e
    u s l u i o i w e d u n
      e r r p m n d r e
        e b e   s
        c s r
        i
        a

Are you lanugo again? Reborn?

***

In these months of masks, I have learned my unbrushed mouth smells like sex:
damp panties, collar bone sweat pools, something under the fingernails.
I am   aroused
and repulsed.
And saddened
that my mouth has done little more than eat food, drink soda, curse at the air.

***

You remember when you feared a plague
plague that eats away at brains and breasts,
cauliflower beauty of overgrown lung
the morning nothing could move—not
Only your heart, bastard betrayer,
you could count until your death.
in the room. Who knows how long

before everyone else did,
like rats at a dumpster, the
pancreas. You remember
your hands, not your toes, not your lungs.
thumped out the seconds
 The brightness of a new day hung
you'd been without air?
Maybe you were lucky at 2:59.

***

Snow is false water. Or ultra- true air.

We'll never shake the feeling of cold here—a cellar, the bottom of a cooler.

We will never be warm again, we say for three weeks.

There are few places on record colder than the shores of Titan's lakes.

JESSE

She was tired of books
telling her how to dress and what to eat,
her big thighs hugging tight
to the orange dinette.
Wasp- waisted girls with their holy skin
and matching breasts made her
want to start peeling her arms,
peeling her skin away
because skin was all it was.

Harold has said he wanted a thin girl
but she never knew he'd been looking
at that high yellow girl down at Abe's store,
thing no bigger than a stick,
freckles and that mixed blood hair,
tried to look sexy anytime a man walked by,
biting her lip until it left a mark,
lighter than pink, but not white
when you got up close.
Why'd he want to go spending time with her?

Because of those tiny breasts
like lemons, he could cover and test
their hardness
and those legs like copper wire
twisting over his back.

Jesse kept telling herself that he'd be back.
Nobody could move like this
and she got up to prove the point,
hitting the corner of the table, hard,
and the chair was kissing her legs again.
That's it, she breathed, watching the cold eggs
slide the plate, the orange juice shimmying
the sides of the glass.

GROTTO

Perhaps, she caught my eye   walking too close to me,
the hairs of her arm crossing   and twining with mine, there because
I'd said we'd lain together before   in that other life she's always talking
about, my thigh partner to the line   of her hip, her breast falling heavy over
her ribcage, that other life she always   wants to get to and drag me with her
fighting but key- eyed and sticky with   wonder, digging
my heels at times, knees locking   waiting for that moment before I
know I would hear the snap   of one then the other and fall into
her, fingers seeking purchase on   what is me and even if my limbs
give, this skin will still find a way   beneath her nails, kneaded
between fingers, laid down in bruised   snaky trails against this growth
of this time, against the image of her   young breasts and down covered
skin and she reaches for me with a hand   like promise and knows that what I'd
said before was dream- talk and berries,   mushrooms and apologies.

FIRST COMMUNION

You have options, now that you're older:

      You may rise from your chair, hands

      on edge, and, Jesusian, flip the table

      in front of you. Or next to you. Why not

      invite others the next time? Someone

      wants to talk about black lives, as if

 you hadn't been trying before now, as

if you ever lived any other, to talk about

this suit, shoulder points slack, center seam

frayed, nubbing, too loose (now) in the seat.

St. Johnette believed second grade Christianity

was too difficult for you—you, the one who knew

Jesus should have been brown, who got a stick

across the back for saying unleavened bread feels

like torn skin, who questioned if we made

this bread to remind us how to hold death

in our hands? To know what a pound of flesh feels

like in the mouth? Difficult was how sharply

the dear bride settled into her white habits.

The lines on the chalk board prepare us for the ticks

of   line-   We   stand   it   s to

the   up.   under   what   mean   be   called.

We never forget who taught us to mark ourselves: teachers,

policemen, the lunch lady taking away your peanut
butter sandwich because the one kid choked on air.

They all ask the same questions:
Where were you?
How did you get there?
Who were you with?
What are you called?

THE PRESIDENT DID NOT WANT TO SEE ANYTHING "DIFFICULT" AT THE NATIONAL MUSEUM OF AFRICAN AMERICAN HISTORY AND CULTURE

August 2019

Bring that boy, David, here. Tell him to put on some clothes; he's just too stupid. When he gets here, hang him from the rafter, iron hooks, just so, an inch from sure footing. After a day of that, put him in the sugar shack with Venus. I DON'T CARE WHICH ONE! But either without arms will put up less of a fight. Bring that here, HERE, here; I need that Klimt to lick the heel of boot. Make him leeeeeeeeeean down; I only want to see the top of his hair. I see your face, boy, she gets this fist in her forehead. It's too loud in here, these other foreign boys—de Kooning, Maderson, de Stael—clashing and shouting. Put them in the back corner, near the drying racks, leave them until the yellow runs like piss down their sturdy frames, 'til they know to quiet down. Strip the Picassos and weave me a shade, and a mat, same for the dogs. Put a roll of those in the outhouse. And did you cut those boys from their supper? You told them what I said would happen if they did it again? Hang a boy on each fence post; it's what they're most afraid of. That aimless boy over there is *not* thinking. Put a fire under him; maybe it'll make him into something useful. But that smug ass Mona girl? Get her from the shack, her sweat should make it easy to wipe her down, get the clothes off her, make her shine. How else are we to know what she's worth if we can't see her breasts?

We agree things happen in repetitious systems.

　　　He argues against cycles, wheeling

　　　his hand in circles before my nose.

　　　I nod my head, feeling my neck pull

　　　to the side following the wand of his arm

　　　with eager wet-dog eyes.

Take for instance he says that every time

　　　I drop this orange on this table

　　　it will not bounce back to my hand.

I have long since stopped saying

　　　that I would not return to that hand-

　　　soft and angry brown, cut with ropes

　　　of hair, not to mention the dropping,

　　　changing heights, places of impact

　　　He has picked up the orange,

　　　thumbed the flat spot, now darker side

　　　and raised his hand again.

Take for instance, for example

　　　that kicking the chair you sit in

　　　I will continue to move the you there

　　　but never where I want you to be

　　　and never where you were.

And he sighs; I think, always a sigh,
Take for instance that I could lean

      here to your face and never

      blink when you do or as often.

Here I would take, *for instance*, that

      his breathing is habit and revolving

      and would argue against it.

MY COUSIN DIES, LIKE A DEER, ON THE SIDE OF THE ROAD

"The Texas Department of Public Safety (DPS) is asking for help from the public in the investigation of a fatal hit-and-run crash that resulted in the death of a pedestrian on FM 160 east of FM 2830. The crash occurred at approximately 11:00 p.m., Sunday June 14." *Bluebonnet News*

You must have been a thing of beauty:
among the hoots, clicks, whistles of swamp-
land dark, then spotlighted, machina-
flung, crescent body, eclipsing, rising—
nyxnaut—occluding white pores in velvet
night nap. Such silence.   all listening
to the luminous staccato, 270 bones, rapturous
vibrato, soul—too long in marrow—released.

No one knows when to applaud.
                              Then:

                                        chirrup

MY MOTHER, WHO IS LOSING HER HEARING,

            has discovered horror movie marathons; the herds of screams
and screwdriver bone scraping solicitor-knock
            on my ear drums while I sleep. I wake panting. Her
laughter plays hide-and-seek from the other room.

            She's annoyed every time the black people
die. But the math works out: There's no Last Girls
            Club for anyone darker than Sherwin Williams
Bungalow Beige, because there is always a new
            girl to bludgeon, to penetrate, to part
–icipate. For every small breasted, tan-skinned girl
            who fades gurgling, pulse throbbing at the well-
oiled neck, two white girls get to live another 35
            minutes. For every blueblack, white-eyed man chain
sawed, a redhead makes it to the last 10 minutes.
            And every time the witch is voodoo brain
wrapped in purple silken scarves, bejeweled fingers
            waving fractured patois, some brown child is shotgunned
while running, neck keepsaked to a bumper like tailgate trophies.

            Mom wants to know why I won't watch with her:
before I leave for the weekly trip to the store
            —eggs, butter, tamales, nuts—she hugs me,
both hands reaching up my back to shoulderblades,
            jutting like wing stumps, says she loves me. If
I close my eyes I see a yellow ribbon bound
            Victory plot of Crotons and Shrimp Plants.

I can't bandwagon in the joyous why
            the teenage wolf isn't snufflesnout into innards;

I am wondering why there isn't a movie where

           the black kids say "No" to the party, gather

instead on the east wall of the cafeteria, not be

           cause they were put there, but because they got

smarter, tried to keep the dumber ones from getting

           in that truck, no one wants to go camping.

The nightly news reports the Nightmare on Elm Street

           house is for sale; the new builds on my block

look little different. Each night the drive is down

           this dark road, ghosts of horse dander, goat dirts,

cow eyelashes. I should be smarter than even having

           this craving to circumnavigate it by the unpolluted

sky. But, there are no other directions for me. The key

           grip has turned away.

Roll credits.

The End.

Goodbye.